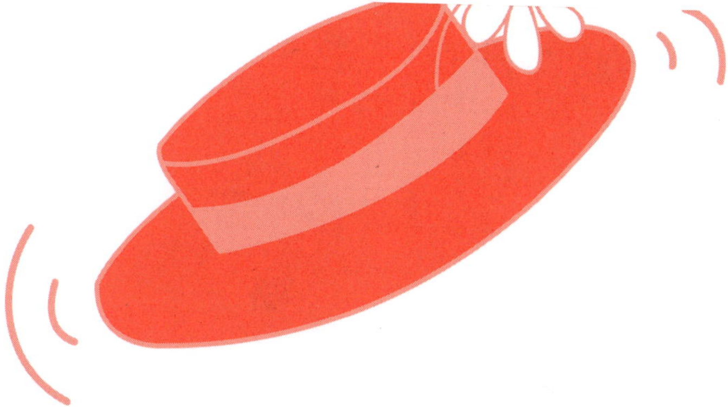

My Red Hattitudes

Jill Larson Sundberg

CONARI PRESS

First published in 2004 by Conari Press,
an imprint of Red Wheel/Weiser, LLC
York Beach, ME
With offices at:
368 Congress Street
Boston, MA 02210
www.redwheelweiser.com

Copyright (c) 2004 Jill Larson Sundberg
All rights reserved. No part of this publication may be reproduced or transmitted in any form or by any means, electronic or mechanical, including photocopying, recording, or by any information storage and retrieval system, without permission in writing from Red Wheel/Weiser, LLC. Reviewers may quote brief passages.

Typeset in ITC Officina Sans, Freestyle Script, and Bermuda LP Squiggle by David A. Freedman.

ISBN 1-57324-203-9

Printed in Canada
FR

11 10 09 08 07 06 05 04
8 7 6 5 4 3 2 1

The paper used in this publication meets the minimum requirements of the American National Standard for Information Sciences-Permanence of Paper for Printed Library Materials Z39.48-1992 (R1997).

Thank you to
Christopher, Angie, Hannah, and Leonard Larson;
David, Ricki, Jonah, and Ally Larson;
and Molly and Joe Galloway
for always including me,
making me feel very special,
and supporting me in my latest ventures.

Thank you, David (my personal CPA),
for all the years you have spent
watching out for me and my business.

And finally, a very special hug for
Laura Payant—welcome to the family.
We are all thrilled to have you!

I love you all very much.

Introduction

We women aged fifty and over are now more independent than ever and we have formed strong bonds with women our own age.

No jobs are out of reach for us baby boomers. As the world turns before our eyes, we are no longer expected to do housework in our dresses and pearls (if we do housework at all). We've traded in our dust mops for briefcases, and we've taught our daughters that women are equal to men. We have now decided to don red hats and wear flashy outfits, attend our Red Hat meetings and discuss doing what we want (and not doing what we don't want).

This idea of independence and breaking from the norm was introduced by very courageous women well before we were born. It was reintroduced recently by Jenny Joseph when she wrote her rather humorous poem "Warning" and emphatically stated that she would "wear purple with a red hat."

Now that my children are grown and the nest is empty, I have decided that it is time to be ME and not worry about hosting graduation parties or carving pumpkins. It's my turn and, yes, I will wear a red hat just to let people know!

With the right attitude,
ANY hat can be worn.

And that, my friend,
is a "hattitude."

I can wear a hat or take it off, but either way, it's a conversation piece.

—Hedda Hopper

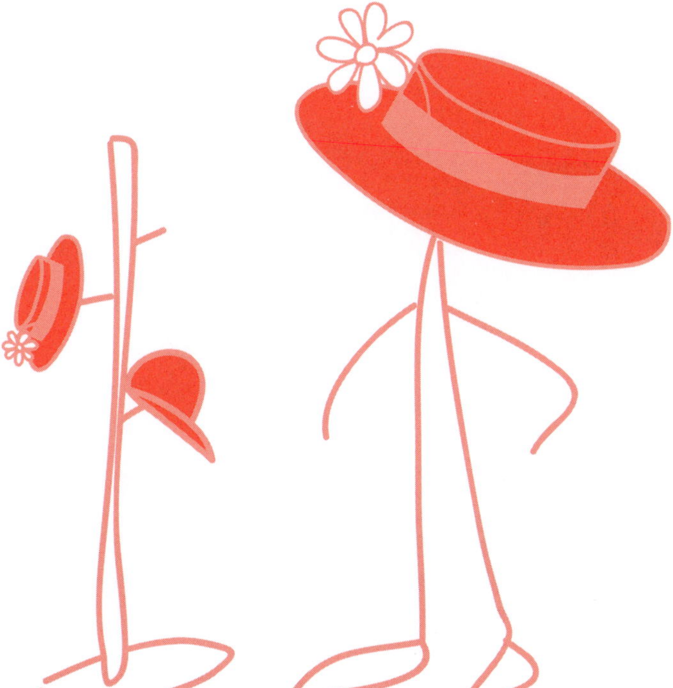

All these years,
people have said,
"Be yourself."

Well, now I'm gonna be!

Just when the caterpillar thought her world was over, she became a butterfly.

*If you want
to live life well,
it helps to maintain
a positive hattitude.*

*Age is a question
of mind over matter.*

*If I don't mind,
it doesn't matter!*

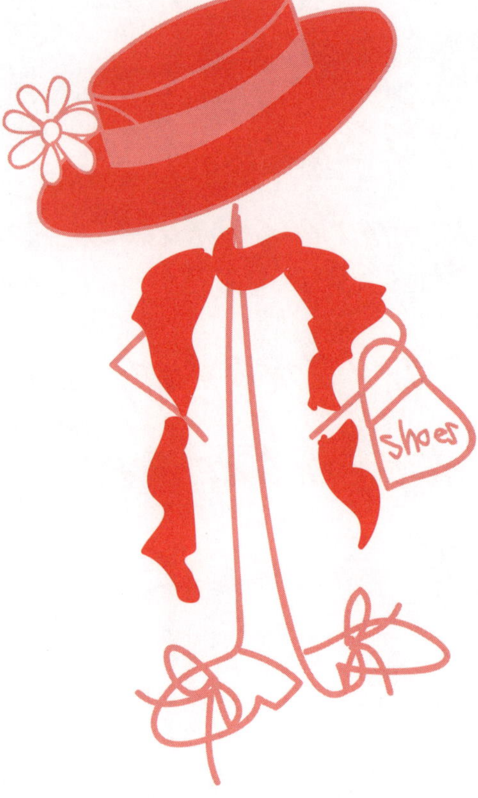
shoes

I can (and I will) wear comfortable shoes.

No more stiletto heels!

Frankly, I think I'm rather cute for my age.

*The secret of staying young
is to love honestly,
eat slowly,
and lie about your age.*

—Lucille Ball

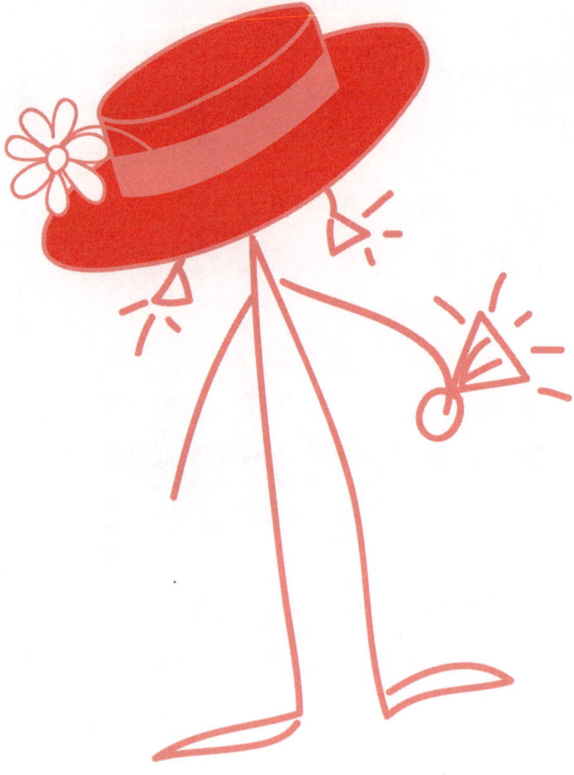

I've always been a big baseball fan.

I absolutely love diamonds.

I am
NOT
falling apart.

Actually, I am
finally getting it together!

Don't wake me . . .

I'm sleeping in.

A woman's hat is her crowning glory.

*My Red Hat
speaks volumes about me
before I speak
a single sentence.*

degree of remarkability

*I think
I'll dare to be remarkable.*

It's not what you wear — it's who you are.

I have hosted my last graduation party.

*I'll have wild tea parties
and invite my friend Alice,
a Red Hatter!*

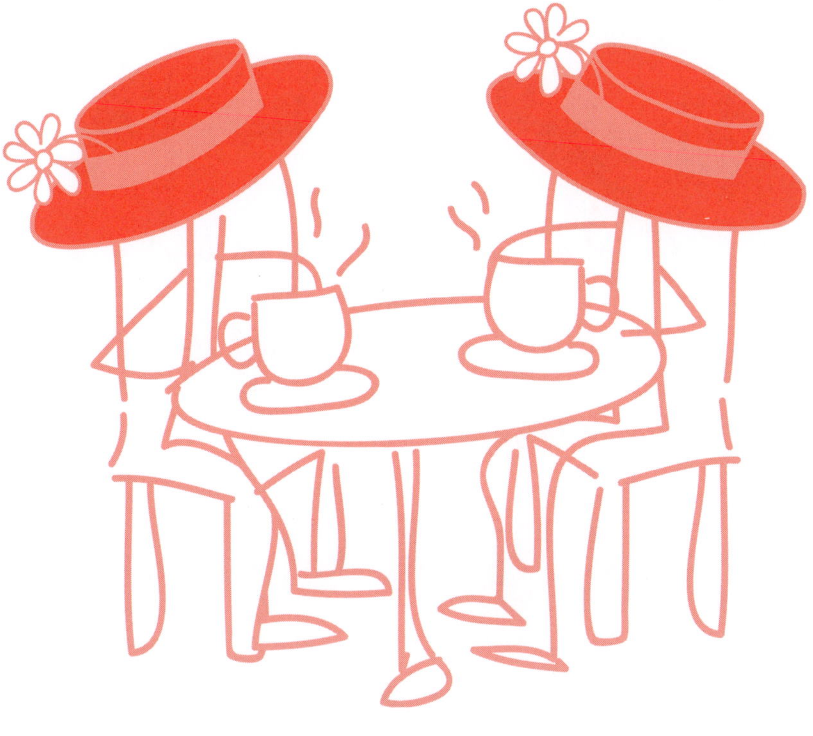

I'll do my best to make sure those who are easily shocked are shocked more often.

*I'm not overweight—
I'm just too short.*

I'm not really bossy —I just have better ideas.

I'll take my senior discount.

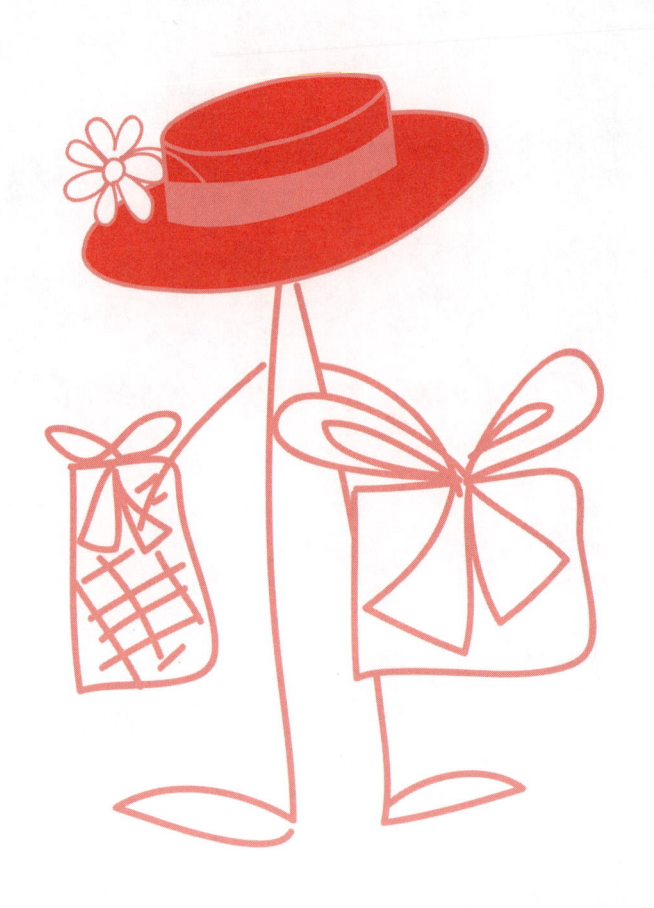

I am definitely going to celebrate every single birthday.

Bring presents!

*Yes,
I will tell you what I think.*

I am no longer going to allow others to control me.

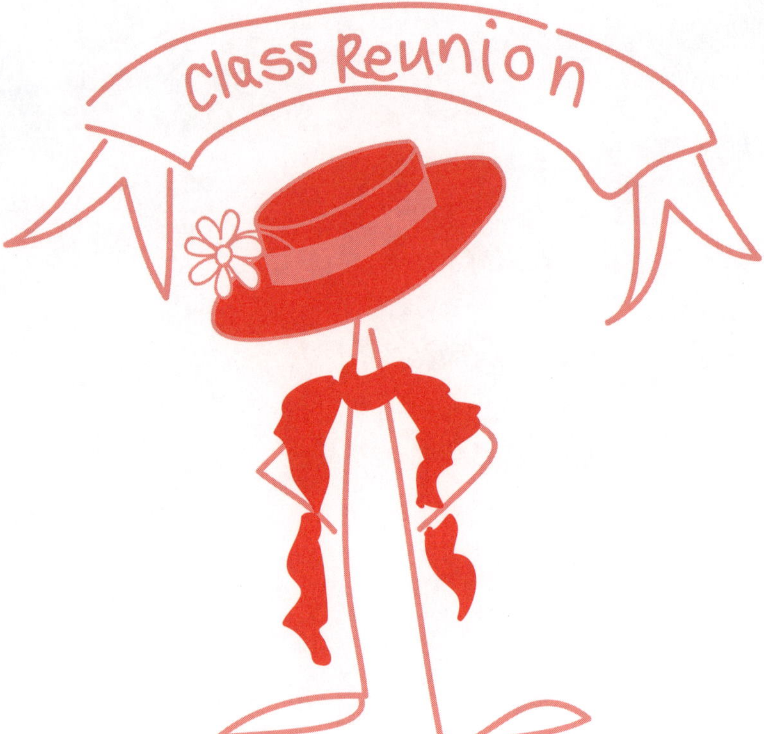
Class Reunion

*By the way,
who were all those old people
at our last class reunion?*

*You are
what others perceive you to be
—until you're 50.*

Then, you can be whatever you darn well please.

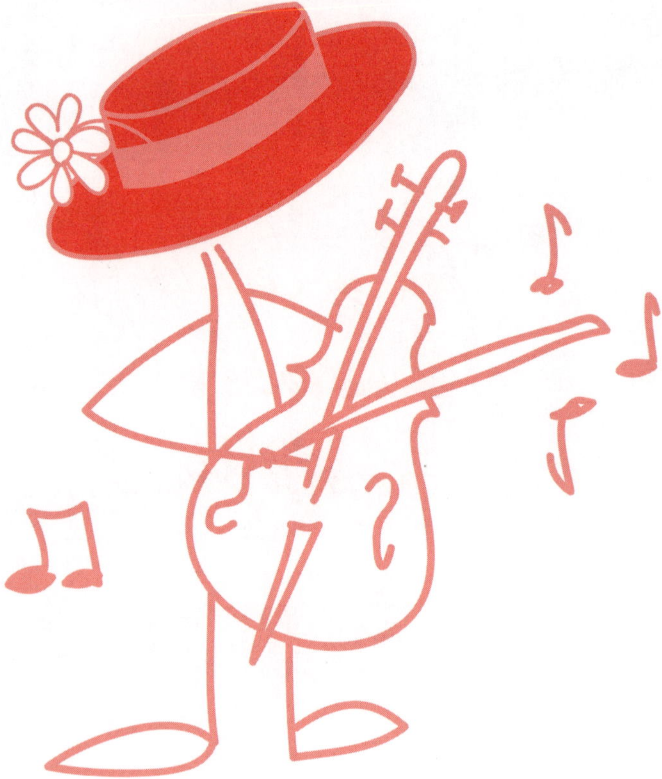

The older the violin, the sweeter the music.

My grandchildren are perfect!

If it feels good, do it.

(If it doesn't, don't!)

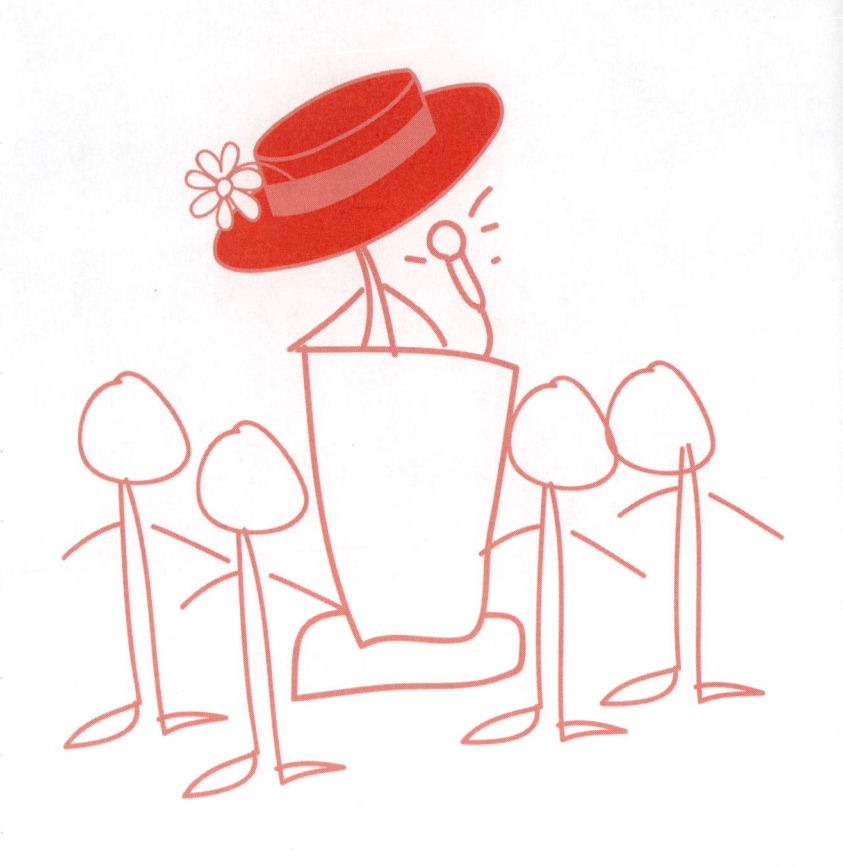

I now realize there is nothing to be afraid of when speaking to a crowd.

I'm keeping my wrinkles —I've earned every single one of them!

I've always been
a people pleaser.

Now it's time to please
ME.

*We're never too old
to begin feeling younger.*

*My mother said
I would never amount to anything
because I always procrastinate.
I said, "Just wait!"*

—Judy Tenuta

I am

NOT

a Domestic Goddess.

Life is too short for me not to kick back and enjoy the ride.

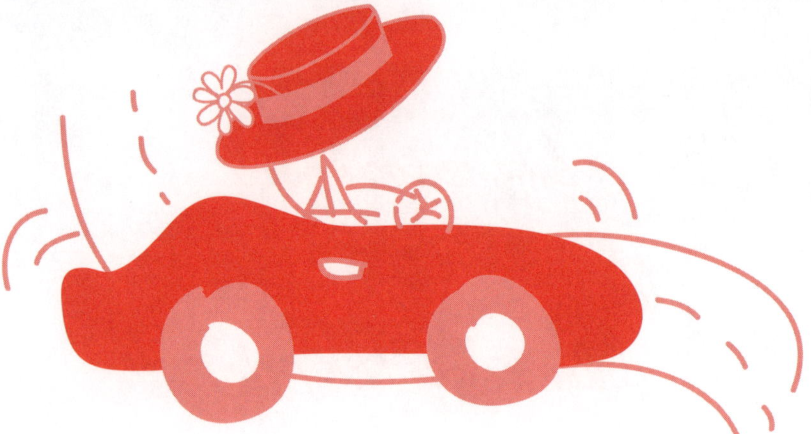

If you're planning to play it safe, you'll want to steer clear of me.

One size does **NOT** fit all!

Don't give me your advice unless I ask for it.

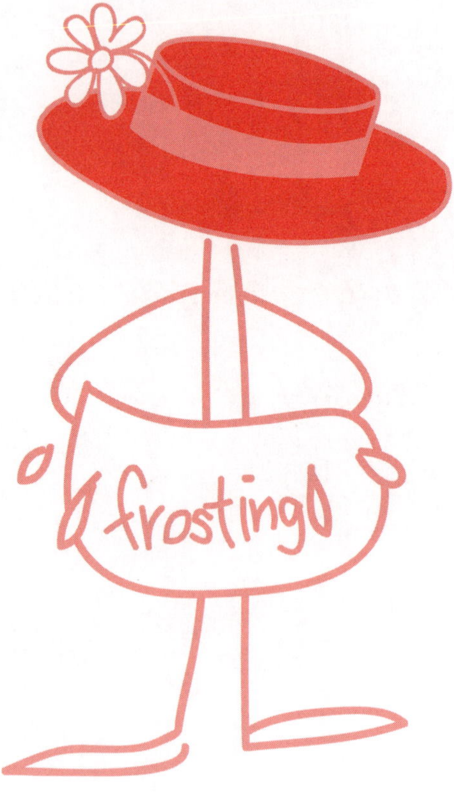
frosting

I'm going to make chocolate frosting and lick the bowl myself.

When I said, "I do,"
I didn't know
I'd be doing everything.

*I will be the life of the party—
but only when I want to be.*

Stages of Life:
Age 20 — I wish I could . . .
Age 30 — I hope I will . . .
Age 40 — I think I can . . .
Age 50 — I know I can . . .
Age 100 — I knew I could.

Girls just wanna have funds.

*I love
tracking down friends
from my past.*

I'm going to be more spontaneous!

I am

NEVER

going to wear horizontal stripes again.

I love hanging out with
my mother and her friends.

They say things like,
"Well, you're just a kid."

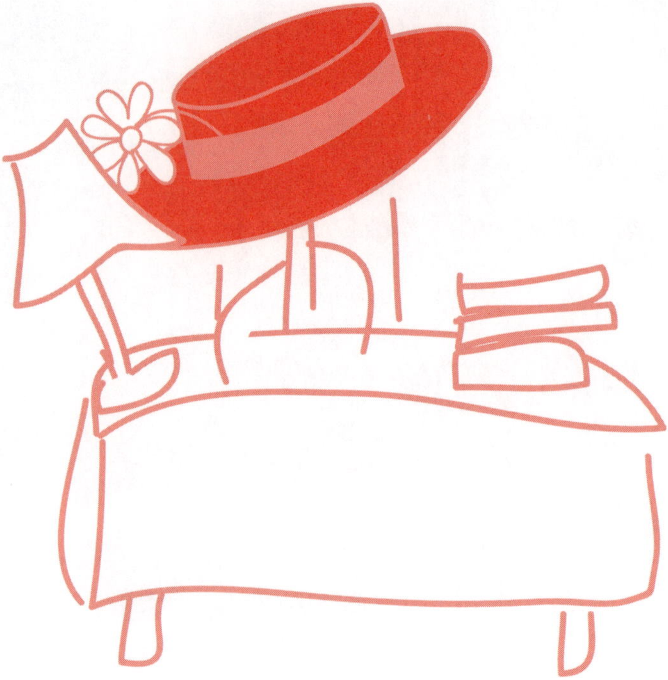

Quit telling me to slow down.

I love my work!

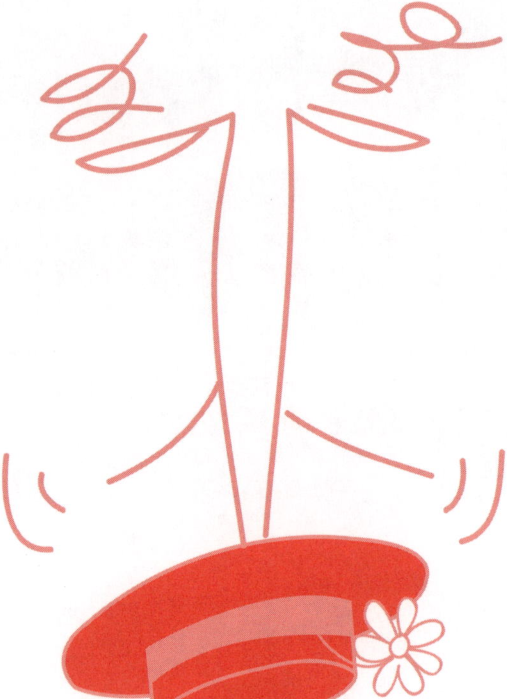

*If I spend all my life
living by the rules,
I'll miss a lot of the fun.*

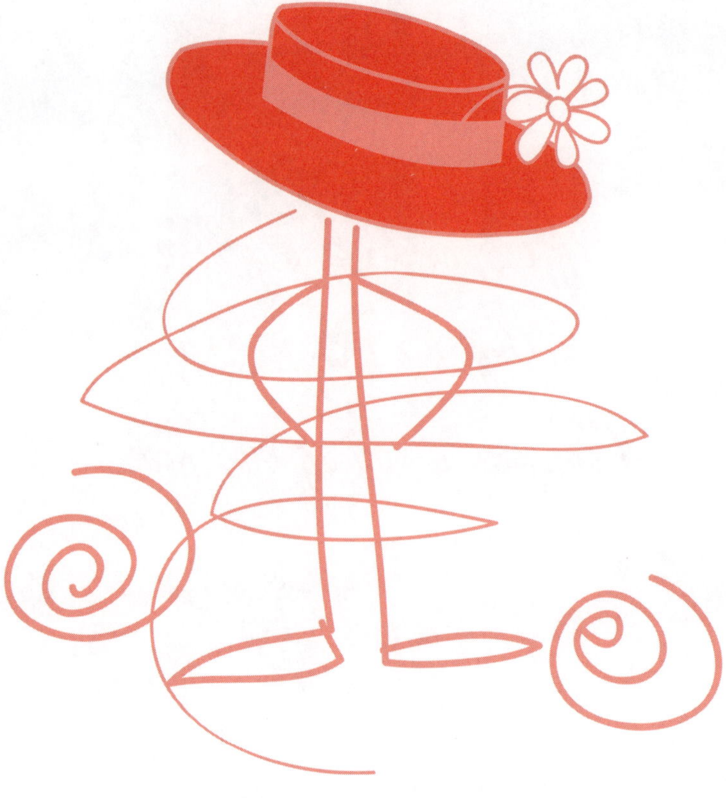

I was told
throughout my childhood that
I was a commotion.

Now I plan
to live up to that reputation!

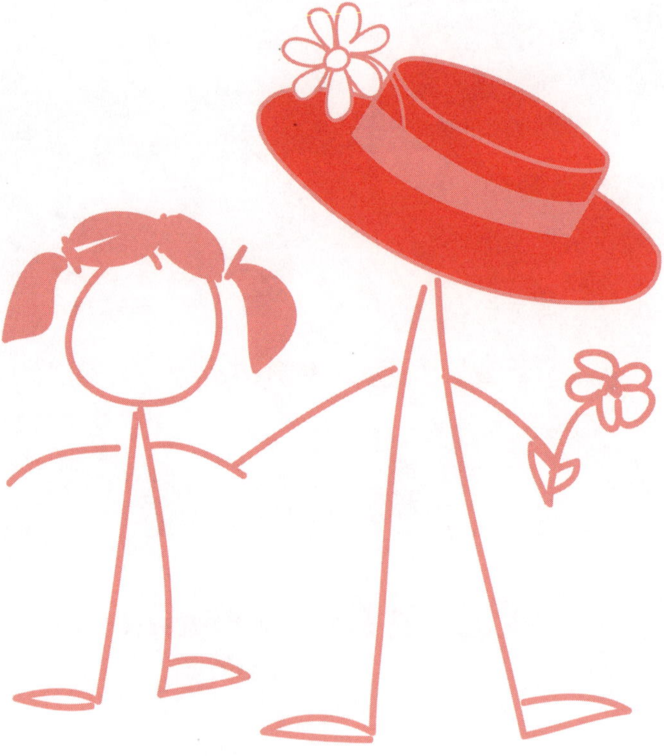

*I'm never too old
to make new friends.*

I never have to eat asparagus again!

*This summer
I'm planning to climb a tree.*

I'm bossy, and I'm adorable.

—Katharine Hepburn

I will paint my house any color I want.

I'm going to hug my friends.

When I was young and rowdy,
my dad would say,
"Just simmer down."

Now, I no longer
have to "simmer down."

I will give more presents.

Aging is a lot like sledding.

It's hard work getting to the top of the hill, but the ride down is the best!

*I'm still a hot chick,
but now it comes in flashes.*

I'm going to walk in the rain without an umbrella.

You are not the boss of me.

I can finally accept offers of help.

I will stand my ground.
I will speak my mind.

I'm no longer going to say yes when I really mean no.

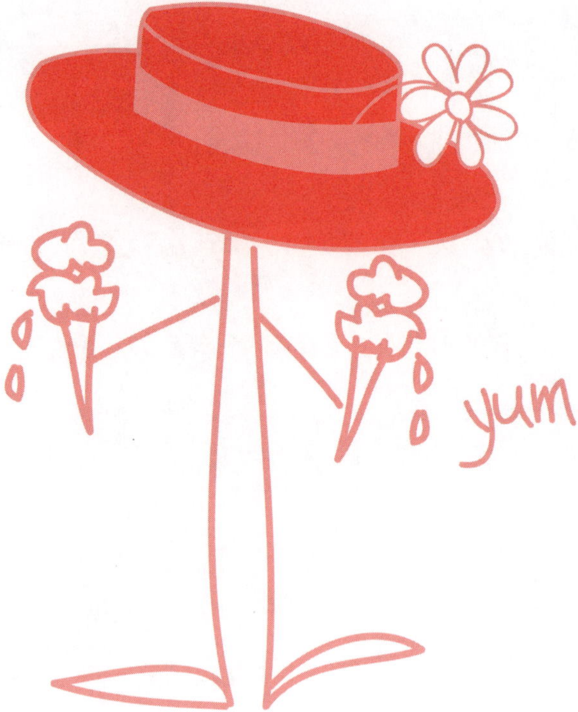
yum

*I will
eat dessert first!*

*You only live once,
but if you do it right,
once is enough.*

—Mae West

*I will live with
the choices I've made,
without regret.*

*I will live my life
to the fullest!*

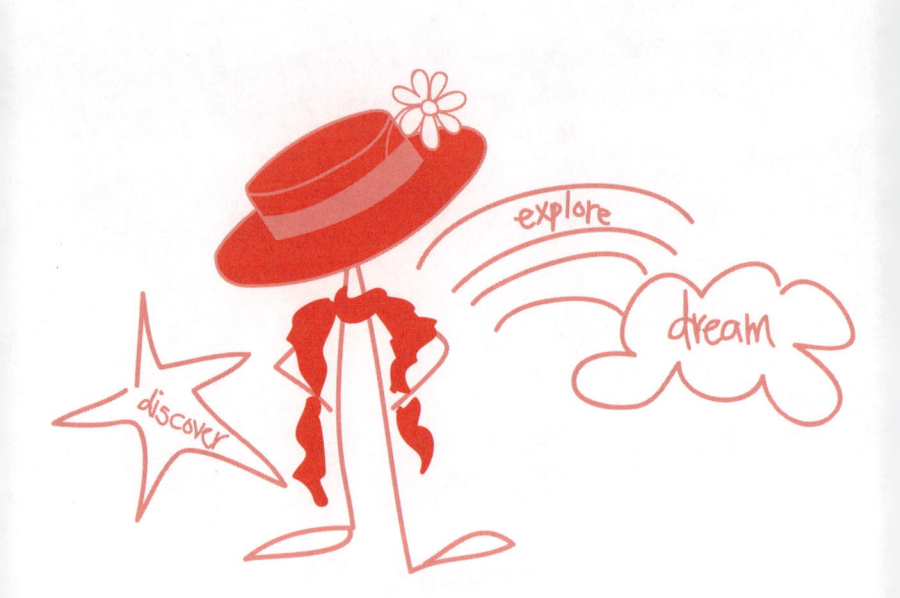
explore
dream
discover

Twenty years from now,
I will be more disappointed by
the things I didn't do
than by the things I did.

Starting today, I will explore,
dream, and discover.

This is as good as it gets!